MISSION TO MARS

THE PATHFINDER MISSION TO MARS

John Hamilton

ABDO
Daughters Publishing

Visit us at
www.abdopub.com

Published by Abdo Publishing Company, 4940 Viking Drive, Edina, Minnesota 55435.

Interior Graphic Design: John Hamilton
Cover Design: MacLean & Tuminelly
Contributing Editor: Alan Gergen

Cover photo: NASA/JPL
Interior photos: NASA/JPL

Sources: Begley, Sharon. *Greetings From Mars*. Newsweek, July 14, 1997, pp. 22-29; Begley, Sharon. *The Stars of Mars*. Newsweek, July 21, 1997, pp. 26-33; Bizony, Piers. *Lost in Space*. Wired, December, 1997, pp. 226-288. Caidin, Martin & Barbree, Jay. *Destination Mars*. New York: Penguin Studio, 1997; Chaikin, Andrew. *Hard Landings*. Air & Space, July, 1997, pp. 48-55; Jet Propulsion Laboratory, Public Information Office, California Institute of Technology, Pasadena, CA; Kluger, Jeffrey. *Uncovering the Secrets of Mars*. Time, July 14, 1997, pp. 26-37; Petersen, Carolyn Collins. *Welcome to Mars*. Sky & Telescope, October, 1997, pp. 34-37; Sagen, Carl. *Cosmos*. New York: Random House, 1980.

Library of Congress Cataloging–in–Publication Data

Hamilton, John, 1959-
    The Pathfinder mission to Mars / John Hamilton
        p. cm. — (Mission to Mars)
    Includes index.
    Summary: Describes the Mars Pathfinder project, in which a vehicle has landed on Mars to investigate the surface of the planet and send back data on Martian geology.
    ISBN 1-56239-831-8
    1. Mars Pathfinder Project (U.S.)—Juvenile literature.   2. Space flight to Mars—Juvenile literature.   3. Mars (Planet)—Exploration—Juvenile literature.
4. Mars probes—Juvenile literature.   [1. Mars Pathfinder Project (U.S.)
2. Space flight to Mars. 3. Mars probes.] I. Title. II. Series: Hamilton, John, 1959-
Mission to Mars.
TL789.8.U6P385   1998
629.43' 543—dc21   97-34704
                                                                    CIP
                                                                    AC

CONTENTS

Chapter 1

The Pathfinder Mission

Imagine you're a creature standing on the surface of Mars (to be specific, the vast flood plain of Ares Vallis in the Northern Hemisphere). Suddenly you hear a sonic boom; something fast is tearing through the thin Martian atmosphere. You look up and notice a fiery streak blazing across the sky. As it nears, a parachute opens, and a section of the object drops down on a long cord. Then, quite suddenly, what looks like a bunch of balloons tied together inflates and encases it.

One hundred feet above the ground, the object drops from the parachute, free-falling toward the red rock- and dust-covered surface. When it hits, it bounces nearly five stories high, then falls back again. Finally, after bounding madly across the surface, the balloon-encased object comes to a rest.

After a few hours, it stirs. The balloons deflate and are pulled underneath. Three silver panels slowly open, like the petals of some weird metallic flower. Inside is a spacecraft, an alien invader from another planet. Except, in this case, the alien planet is Earth.

Facing page: Cushioned by an array of airbags, *Pathfinder* lands on the surface of Mars.

4

On July 4, 1997, the citizens of Earth once again made their mark on Mars. Not since the Viking missions of 1976 have we sent a probe to that remote, forbidding planet. This time the spacecraft's name was *Pathfinder*. Once again Mars captured the imagination of humanity. On the day of the landing, NASA's *Pathfinder* World Wide Web site scored over 100 million "hits." People were glued to their televisions as *Pathfinder*'s micro rover, named *Sojourner*, slowly crept over the reddish Martian soil. As President Bill Clinton said, "Our return to Mars today marks the beginning of a new era in the nation's space-exploration program."

An image of Mars as seen by the *Viking 1* orbiter.

CHAPTER 2

• • • • • • • • • • • • • • •

A New NASA

America's return to Mars came on the heels of a budgetary shakedown at the National Aeronautics and Space Administration (NASA). After decades of launching huge, multi-billion dollar space systems, the space agency began to feel the same budget pinch under which the rest of the country was reeling. By the early 1990s, the Cold War was over. This competition with the Soviet Union had fueled the drive—and funding—for much of our space program, especially the race to the moon. But in today's budget-conscious atmosphere, it became harder and harder to justify spending billions of dollars on every space flight.

In the golden age of NASA, back in the 1970s and 1980s, it was common for space probes (like Pioneer, Voyager, or Viking) to be crammed with every science experiment possible. Backup systems were common, so that if one experiment failed, its backup could take over. This, of course, made the probes more expensive. (Both Viking missions to Mars in 1976 cost the American public about $3 billion in today's dollars.) But NASA planners wanted to make sure the missions succeeded no matter what might go wrong. The trouble is, sometimes things go wrong—spacecraft crash on liftoff, or get lost in space—no matter how many backup plans you have.

In 1993, NASA's *Mars Observer* spacecraft was due to enter orbit around the Red Planet and begin taking high-resolution photographs. It was a complicated piece of machinery, packed with state-of-the-art high technology. Just before the probe entered orbit, a fuel line burst, sending *Observer* spinning uselessly into deep space, where it was lost forever, to the tune of nearly $1 billion.

When NASA Administrator Daniel Goldin took over in 1992, it was clear to him that the bloated space agency had to be downsized, just as other areas of government were being trimmed. The loss of the expensive *Observer* spacecraft made that obvious. Under Goldin's direction, NASA embraced a new philosophy. Instead of designing big, expensive spacecraft that needed years of planning and hundreds of scientists, NASA would build many less expensive, more streamlined probes instead. As Goldin

A mockup of a Viking lander.

said, NASA planetary missions would now become, "better, faster, cheaper." Said NASA Associate Administrator for Space Science Dr. Wesley T. Huntress Jr., "We've turned the old way of doing business upside down."

The *Mars Pathfinder* mission would be one of the first projects in this new design philosophy, which is called the Discovery Program. It would quickly be followed by the *Mars Global Surveyor* mission, which is scheduled to begin detailed mapping of the Red Planet during the spring of 1999. Following that will be up to eight other probes, leading to a possible manned mission during the first part of the next century.

But first, NASA had to prove that *Pathfinder* could do the job.

The *Mars Global Surveyor* mission is scheduled to start mapping Mars in the spring of 1999.

CHAPTER 3

· · · · · · · · · · · · · ·

SPACECRAFT DESIGN ON A SHOESTRING

The Discovery Program, with its "better, faster, cheaper" motto, gives each planetary probe mission a budget cap of about $150 million. For a space mission, this isn't very much money. (Compare it to the cost of an average Space Shuttle launch, which has a price tag of around $350 million.) Only science projects absolutely necessary for a mission are included. Each mission uses a handful of engineers from NASA's Jet Propulsion Laboratory (JPL), not the staff of hundreds as on previous missions. Time is speeded up also—two or three years are budgeted to complete a project, instead of a decade.

The *Pathfinder* mission had a simple goal: test the performance of a rover in the hostile environment of Mars. The rover, a six-wheeled robot about the size of a big skateboard, was named *Sojourner*, after the U.S. Civil War abolitionist Sojourner Truth. (The word sojourner means "traveler.")

Sojourner had cleats on each wheel to give it traction in the dusty Martian soil, and could navigate at a top speed of up to 0.4 inches per second. A solar panel on top gave it power, while five lasers would help controllers on Earth identify obstacles in its path. Two front-mounted black-and-white cameras took stereo pictures, while a special device called an "Alpha proton X-ray spectrometer" identified the kinds of rocks and soil the rover would find on its mission.

In addition to its main goal, *Pathfinder* would also have to prove that new technologies used to get to the planet's surface could be used in future lander missions. The mission would also perform science experiments by analyzing Martian soil and rocks, and taking weather measurements.

The handful of engineers assigned to getting the rover to Mars were faced with a tough task. Many scientists didn't think it could be done for so little money. But many of the engineers on the team were young and ambitious.

NASA technicians perform a final check on *Sojourner*.

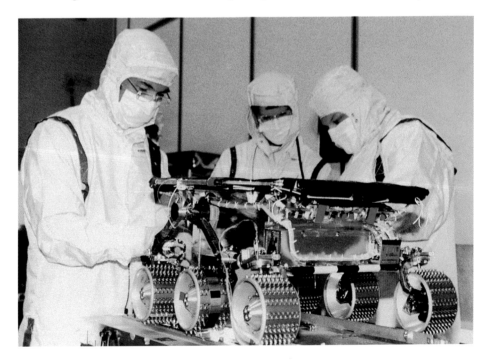

What they lacked in funding they made up for with hard work and ingenuity.

To save money, the *Pathfinder* team used a lot of electronic components that already existed, or were slightly modified. For example, two radio modems that were needed to communicate with the rover were bought from the Motorola company for $2,000 each, then modified for the mission. *Pathfinder*'s heatshield design, used to protect the spacecraft from the intense heat of dropping through the Martian atmosphere, was taken from the earlier Viking missions.

Unlike the Viking missions, the *Pathfinder* team did not have to worry about sterilizing the lander equipment. Sterilization gobbled up nearly one fourth of Viking's $3 billion budget. Besides, scientists analyzing data sent from the Viking landers decided that no microorganism from Earth could survive on Mars. The atmosphere is hostile to live organisms; it's a freezing-cold, bone dry place, with deadly ultraviolet radiation from the sun constantly bombarding the planet's surface.

Another major cost saving would be in how the spacecraft actually landed on the planet. Instead of Viking- or Apollo-style retrorockets firing to provide a soft landing (rockets and extra fuel are expensive), *Pathfinder* would simply drop down on the surface. The team decided not even to orbit Mars first, like every other lander probe had done. *Pathfinder* would simply catch up to Mars after chasing it for 6.5 months and 310 million miles (496 million km), then drop into the planet's atmosphere.

Retrorockets would fire briefly to slow the spacecraft down before it began its fiery entry into the thin Martian

The fully assembled *Pathfinder* spacecraft mated to the third-stage rocket booster.

atmosphere. A parachute would deploy, and then four giant airbags would inflate, enveloping the 800-pound (360-kg) lander and cushioning it as it impacted the surface at an estimated speed of 60 miles per hour (96 km per hour). At least that was the plan—making it work would require a lot of ingenuity and testing.

The airbags were the most difficult part of the mission to get right. The idea itself had been considered by NASA back in the 1960s. Now the *Pathfinder* team had to make the idea work, on time and under budget.

First they chose a lightweight fabric called Vectran, an extremely strong cloth similar to Kevlar, which is used to make bulletproof vests. Unfortunately, Vectran isn't easy to sew. Errors in the seams caused the airbags to rip apart when they were inflated. When that problem was solved, the *Pathfinder* team tried out the airbags in a special "Mars Yard" designed to simulate the surface of Mars, complete with rocks and red soil. When the airbags were dragged across the sharp rocks (as if the wind were dragging the spacecraft across the surface) they were ripped to shreds. Finally, multiple layers of Vectran were used to solve the ripping problem. After finding a way to pack the airbags into the cramped spacecraft, *Pathfinder* was ready for liftoff.

An airbag inflation test is performed at *Pathfinder's* "Mars Yard" test site.

. . . .

CHAPTER 4

THE JOURNEY TO MARS

Every 26 months, Earth and Mars are close enough together to make travel practical. *Pathfinder* began its journey on December 4, 1996. The flight system sat atop a Delta II rocket, which was launched from Cape Canaveral, Florida.

Pathfinder blasts off toward Mars atop a Delta II rocket.

Pathfinder began a long, arching path through space to catch up with the Red Planet, which of course was also travelling through space on its path around the sun. When *Pathfinder* caught up with Mars, the two planets were 119 million miles (190.4 million km) apart, but the spacecraft had traveled over 310 million miles (496 million km).

The mission's guidance system was amazingly accurate, making only four mid-course corrections on the long journey. And since there were no plans to orbit Mars first, *Pathfinder* had to enter the planet's atmosphere at just the right angle, even though it was zooming in at over 16,000 miles (25,600 km) per hour. If it came in too shallow (hitting a glancing blow) the spacecraft would skip off the atmosphere and be hurled far into deep space. Too steep, and it would crash onto the surface. NASA explained it like this: *Pathfinder* landing on Mars was like hitting a golf ball onto a green less than a foot wide, at a distance from Pasadena, CA, to Atlanta, GA.

On July 4, 1997, *Pathfinder* finally entered Mars' atmosphere, just under the proper angle. Even though Mars' atmosphere is very thin compared to Earth, it was still enough to slow *Pathfinder* down to about 900 miles (1,440 km) per hour. Guarded by its heatshield, the spacecraft blazed a fiery trail across the pink Martian sky. Six miles (9.6 km) above the surface, a huge, 24-foot (7.3-meter) parachute opened, slowing the spacecraft down to about 220 miles (352 km) per hour. A few seconds later, the heatshield was discarded.

Directly below *Pathfinder* lay its target—Ares Vallis, a wide floodplain at the mouth of a major canyon system. At one time, scientists say, a flood of water equal in volume to all five of Earth's Great Lakes washed through this now-dry valley. Because of this monumental flooding, scientists expected rocks of all sorts to be strewn across the valley. In effect, *Pathfinder* would sample many different spots on Mars and only have to be in one place to do it.

The *Pathfinder* cruise stage approaches Mars.

Pathfinder descends to the surface of the Red Planet.

Eighty seconds from touchdown, at about 16,000 feet (4,850 meters) from the surface, the main lander separated from the entry vehicle on a long tether made of tough Kevlar fabric. From that point, the probe used a radar system to gauge its distance from the surface. At just under 300 feet (91 meters) in altitude, *Pathfinder*'s four giant airbags inflated, protecting the probe from the impact to come.

Four seconds before impact, retrorockets fired for a brief two-second burst, which slowed the probe down to a hover. At that point, the tether was cut, and *Pathfinder* dropped to the surface from a height of 100 feet (30.3 meters).

When it hit, the airbags worked perfectly, protecting the precious cargo inside. The probe bounced nearly 50 feet (15.2 meters) high, then fell to the ground again. For a minute and a half *Pathfinder* bounded across the Martian surface until, finally, it settled to a stop on the frigid plain of Ares Vallis.

For the first time in 21 years, humans had made their mark on Mars once again.

Entry into Mars'
atmosphere,
five minutes to
touchdown.

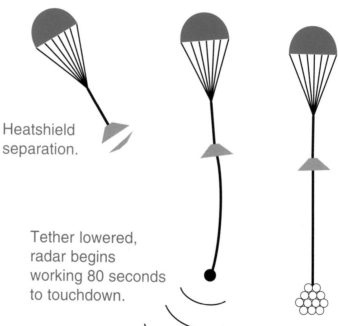

Mars at
launch

Earth

Launch
Dec. 4, 1996

Arrives
July 4, 1997

Parachute deployed,
6 miles (9.6 km)
from surface, two
minutes to
touchdown.

Heatshield
separation.

Tether lowered,
radar begins
working 80 seconds
to touchdown.

Airbags inflate,
294 feet (89 m).

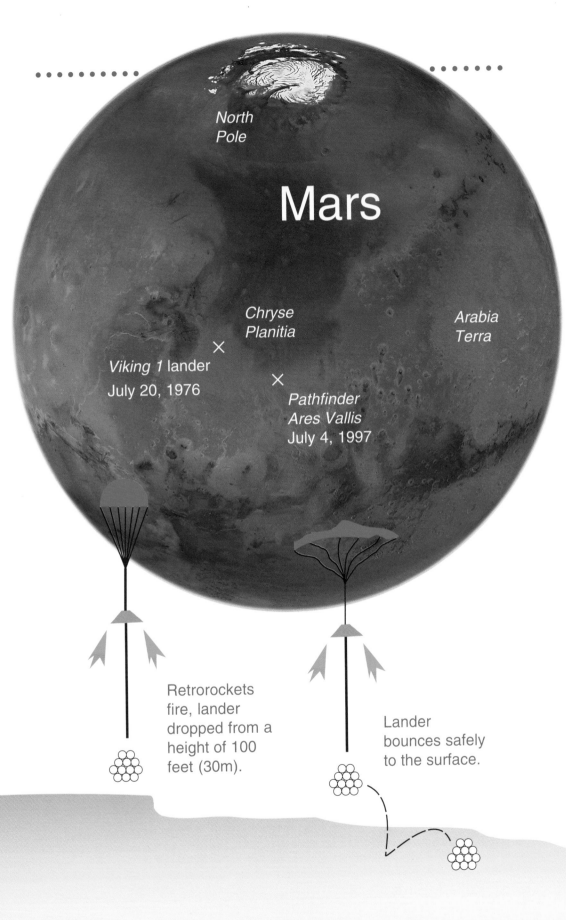

Mars

North Pole

Chryse Planitia

Arabia Terra

Viking 1 lander
July 20, 1976

Pathfinder
Ares Vallis
July 4, 1997

Retrorockets fire, lander dropped from a height of 100 feet (30m).

Lander bounces safely to the surface.

CHAPTER 5
. . . .
THE ARRIVAL

The *Pathfinder* team had fully expected the probe to come to a rest upside down, or on its side. It was designed so it could flip itself right side up. But luck was with *Pathfinder;* it came to a rest in an upright position. The airbags deflated and the probe's three solar panels opened like a big metallic flower. Rays from the sun began powering the probe's instruments. Scientists at NASA were overjoyed at their success.

The landing wasn't completely without trouble, though. Computers aboard *Pathfinder* and *Sojourner* were having trouble "talking" to one another, which prevented the rover from getting instructions it needed to begin exploring the landing site.

A bigger problem was soon revealed when the airbags deflated. Motors in the lander slowly drew the spent airbags underneath and out of the way. But one of the airbags got stuck, preventing *Sojourner* from driving down its ramp to the Martian surface. NASA had thought this might happen, though, and the mission team soon went to work fixing the problem. One of the petal-shaped solar panels was repeatedly raised and lowered, which pushed the airbag aside enough for *Sojourner* to move down the ramp. Soon, the computer problem was fixed also, giving a green light for *Sojourner* to begin its mission.

Pathfinder makes its final descent to the Martian surface.

Pathfinder sent back its first weather report: the temperature on Ares Vallis was a bone-chilling –64 degrees Fahrenheit (–53 degrees Celsius). The spacecraft was built to withstand such cold for at least 30 Sols, or Mars days. (Each Mars day equals 24 hours, 40 minutes.)

Pathfinder raised its high-resolution camera to a height of about 5 feet (1.5 meters) and began sending images back to Earth, first in black-and-white, and then in panoramic high-resolution color. The pictures of the Martian surface were stunning in their detail.

The landscape looked almost like a scene from the American Southwest, but without any cactus or sagebrush. The rust-colored soil was littered with rocks and boulders of every shape and size. One boulder close to the lander resembled a cartoon character, and was promptly dubbed "Yogi." Off in the distance, under a salmon-colored sky,

The *Sojourner* rover and undeployed ramps onboard the *Pathfinder* spacecraft. This image was taken on July 4, 1997, shortly after landing on Mars.

"Twin Peaks" loom in the distance as *Sojourner* prepares to venture onto the Martian surface.

two mountains loomed on the horizon. The *Pathfinder* team called these features "Twin Peaks." A big crater lay a mere mile or two away. It was lucky *Pathfinder* did not land in the crater, since it surely would have made the mission much more difficult.

In time, *Pathfinder* began transmitting color images in stereo. When NASA scientists looked at the photos with special red-and-blue glasses, they saw the Martian terrain in 3D.

The *Carl Sagan Memorial Station* as seen by the *Sojourner* rover.

NASA later announced that it had renamed the *Pathfinder* spacecraft the *Carl Sagan Memorial Station*. Carl Sagan was a popular astronomer and space scientist who had died earlier in 1997. His work greatly helped the push toward getting spacecraft to Mars, and he will be sorely missed. Renaming *Pathfinder* in his honor was a fitting tribute to his important contributions.

CHAPTER 6
. . . .
SOJOURNER

Finally, the stage was set for *Sojourner*. The microwave oven-sized rover rolled down its ramp onto the Martian soil without any problems. It was headed for its first objective: a medium-sized blue-gray rock NASA called "Barnacle Bill," which was about 9 feet (2.7 meters) away from the lander.

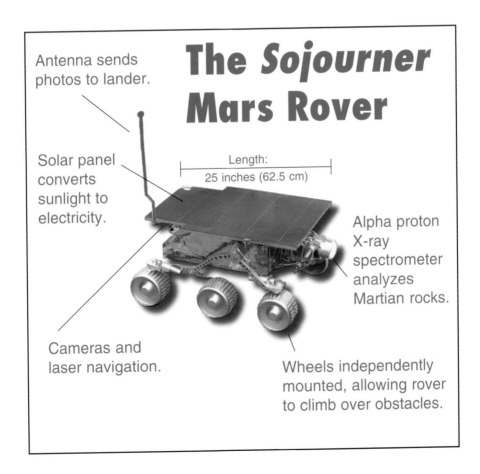

The *Sojourner* Mars Rover

Antenna sends photos to lander.

Solar panel converts sunlight to electricity.

Length: 25 inches (62.5 cm)

Alpha proton X-ray spectrometer analyzes Martian rocks.

Cameras and laser navigation.

Wheels independently mounted, allowing rover to climb over obstacles.

Sojourner measured about 2 feet (.6 meter) long, 1.5 feet (.45 meter) wide, and 1 foot (.3 meter) high. It weighed 22 pounds (9.9 kg), and was powered by a flat solar array sitting on top. The rover moved very slowly, about 2 feet (.6 meter) per minute. It got its instructions from controllers back on Earth. But operating *Sojourner* wasn't exactly like playing with a radio-controlled model car. Since the two planets were 119 million miles (190.4 million km) apart, signals took 11 minutes to get to Mars, even though they were travelling at the speed of light. Controllers back on Earth had to carefully tell the rover how far to go and in which direction. Sometimes *Sojourner* ran across large rocks, but its six metal-cleated wheels moved independently of each other, which usually kept

it from getting stuck. It was like a little sport utility vehicle on Mars.

When *Sojourner* reached Barnacle Bill, it reached out slowly with its X-ray spectrometer. For 10 hours the rover took measurements of the rock, faithfully transmitting digital data to the lander, which relayed it back to Earth. After studying Barnacle Bill, the rover moved on to its next goal, the large boulder called Yogi.

In addition to analyzing rocks, *Sojourner* took pictures using both stereoscopic black-and-white and single-lens color cameras. Some of the pictures were quite stunning. One showed the lander, its solar panels spread open, with tracks running all around it—tracks from *Sojourner* itself, the mark of humankind in the Martian dust.

Sojourner places its X-ray spectrometer on the large Martian boulder named Yogi.

CHAPTER 7

· · · · · · · · · · · · · · ·

A PHENOMENAL MISSION

The *Sagan Memorial Station* was designed to last 30 Martian days; the rover had an expected lifetime of 7. But it wasn't until October 6, 1997, that NASA finally lost contact with the lander. It had lasted three times its expected lifetime. In the end, the harsh conditions on Mars, quite probably the bone-chilling cold, forced silence upon *Pathfinder*.

Since its landing on July 4, 1997, the *Pathfinder* mission sent back more than 16,000 images from the lander and 550 images from the rover. It also sent more than 15 chemical analyses of rocks, plus information on Mars' wind and weather patterns.

Some science highlights:

- Martian dust includes magnetic particles, with a size of about one micron.
- The soil chemistry of Ares Vallis is very similar to that found at the *Viking 1* and *2* landing sites.
- Many "dust devils" were found, caused by frequent wind gusts. These gusts may explain how so much dust gets into Mars' atmosphere.

The weather patterns recorded by *Pathfinder* were similar to those found by *Viking 1*. There were rapid pressure and temperature variations.

Rounded pebbles and rocks, usually formed in running water, were found on the ground. Geologists say this confirms that Mars, during its ancient past, once had a lot of liquid water present.

A map of *Pathfinder's* location on Mars, made by using images from the Viking orbiters.

All in all, the *Pathfinder* mission was an outstanding achievement. Said NASA Administrator Dan Goldin, "I want to thank the many talented men and women at NASA for making the mission such a phenomenal success. It embodies the spirit of NASA, and serves as a model for future missions that are faster, better, and cheaper. Today, NASA's *Pathfinder* team should take a bow, because America is giving them a standing ovation for a stellar performance."

Dr. David Baltimore, president of the California Institute of Technology, which manages JPL for NASA, said, "This mission has advanced our knowledge of Mars tremendously, and will surely be a beacon of success for upcoming missions to the Red Planet. Done quickly and within a very limited budget, *Pathfinder* sets a standard for twenty-first century space exploration."

A Martian sunset as seen by *Pathfinder*.

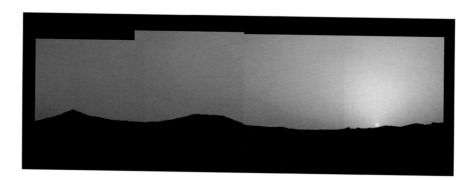

INTERNET SITES

Starchild: A learning center for young astronomers
http://starchild.gsfc.nasa.gov/

This lively site, a service of the Laboratory for High Energy Astrophysics at NASA, is full of information on the solar system, astronauts, and space travel. It has a very good section on Mars covering the main features of the Red Planet, including photos.

Mars Missions
http://mpfwww.jpl.nasa.gov/

This NASA web page provides up-to-the-minute information and photographs on three current space probes: *Mars Pathfinder*, *Mars Global Surveyor*, and *Mars Surveyor 98*.

The Whole Mars Catalog
http://www.reston.com/astro/mars/catalog.html

This is a very extensive site of Mars facts and photos, with many links to other related web sites. Some of the many topics include Mars facts, breaking news from NASA, space probes, and the push to put humans on Mars.

These sites are subject to change. Go to your favorite search engine and type in "Mars" for more sites.

PASS IT ON

Space buffs: educate readers around the country by passing on information you've learned about Mars and space exploration. Share your little-known facts and interesting stories. We want to hear from you!

To get posted on the ABDO & Daughters website, E-mail us at "Science@abdopub.com"

Visit the ABDO & Daughters website at www.abdopub.com

GLOSSARY

· · · · · · · · · · · · · · · · ·

probe

A probe is an unmanned space vehicle that is sent on missions that are too dangerous, or would take too long, for human astronauts to accomplish. Probes are equipped with many scientific instruments, like cameras and radiation detectors. Information from these instruments is radioed back to ground controllers on Earth.

rocket

A vehicle that moves because of the ejection of gases made by the burning of a self-contained propellant. The propellant is made up of fuel, like liquid hydrogen, and an oxidant like liquid oxygen, which helps the fuel to burn. Sometimes solid explosives are used, like nitroglycerin and nitrocellulose. Solid-fuel rockets are more reliable, but generate less thrust. Some spacecraft, like the United States' Space Shuttle, use a combination of solid and liquid fuel rocket boosters. Rockets were probably invented by the Chinese almost 1,000 years ago, when they stuffed gunpowder into bamboo pipes to make weapons.

solar panel

Many space probes use solar panels, which are large arrays of connected solar cells, to generate electricity. Solar cells are semiconductor devices that convert the energy of sunlight into electric energy. Electricity is needed to power the probe's science experiments, guidance systems, and radios. Some probes, especially those that travel far from the sun to explore the outer planets, rely on internal nuclear power plants to generate electricity. The Cassini probe to Saturn, launched in October of 1997 and due to arrive in 2004, uses a nuclear generator.

solar system

The sun, the nine planets, and other celestial bodies (like asteroids) that orbit the sun. The nine planets are (in order from the sun): Mercury, Venus, Earth, Mars, Jupiter, Saturn, Uranus, Neptune, and Pluto.

spectrometer

An instrument that determines what an unknown object is made of by analyzing how it reacts to the bombardment of an "energy spectrum," like heat or X-rays. Each of the known elements has its own special spectrum "signature," so by comparing these to the results of a spectrometer we can tell the chemical makeup of an unknown object.

star

A large, self-containing ball of gas that is "self luminous," or emits light. Stars come in many sizes, ranging from white dwarfs to red giants. The sun is a medium-sized yellow star. At night, stars are seen as twinkling points of light, which is one way to tell them apart from planets, which do not twinkle.

telescope

A device to detect and observe distant objects by their reflection or emission of various kinds of electromagnetic radiation (like light). Most astronomy research today is conducted with telescopes that detect electromagnetic radiation other than visible light, such as radio or x-ray telescopes.

INDEX